Girls
wanna have fun!

D0599113

FRIENDSHIP
Crafts

By Francesca Rusackas

Illustrated by Charlene Olexiewicz

LOWELL HOUSE JUVENILE

LOS ANGELES

NTC/Contemporary Publishing Group

To my mother, Bobette Wright,
for showing me the many ways to share fun!
—F.R.

Published by Lowell House
A division of NTC/Contemporary Publishing Group, Inc.
4255 West Touhy Avenue, Lincolnwood (Chicago), Illinois 60646-1975 U.S.A.

Requests for such permissions should be addressed to:
NTC/Contemporary Publishing Group, Inc.
4255 West Touhy Avenue, Lincolnwood (Chicago), Illinois 60646-1975 U.S.A.

Managing Director and Publisher: Jack Artenstein
Director of Publishing Services: Rena Copperman
Editorial Director: Brenda Pope-Ostrow
Director of Juvenile Development: Amy Downing
Designer: Treesha R. Vaux
Cover Craft: Francesca Rusackas
Cover Photograph: Ann Bogart

Library of Congress Catalog Card Number: 98-75610

ISBN 0-7373-0641-6

Lowell House books can be purchased at special discounts when ordered in bulk for premiums and special sales.
Contact Customer Service at the above address, or call 1-800-323-4900.

Manufactured in the United States of America

RDD 10 9 8 7 6 5 4 3 2 1

Contents

✿ Mobile-ize Your Pals ✿

This picturesque mobile will remind your buddies
of all that they can be.

You Need

• wire cutters • two wire clothes hangers • masking tape • newspaper
• paper plate • acrylic paint (you choose the color) • sponge brush
• people-oriented magazine • scissors • craft glue • various colors of poster board
• color photos of you and your friends • string • transparent tape

Directions

1. Use wire cutters to carefully cut the hooked end off one of the wire hangers. Slip the hookless hanger inside the other hanger, creating an *X*.

2. Turn the hangers over so the remaining hook is on the bottom. Working from the top, wrap the masking tape around the two wire hangers where they form an *X*. Keep wrapping until the hangers are securely joined.

3. Turn the hangers over so the hook is now back on top. Secure the top side of the hangers by wrapping the center of the two wire hangers at the base of the hook with the masking tape.

4. Now get ready to paint the frame of your mobile. First, spread newspaper over your work area. Then pour a small amount of paint onto the paper plate. Use the sponge brush to paint both the hangers and the tape. Let dry for one hour.

5. While you're waiting, go through a magazine and look for pictures of people doing fun and interesting things. Cut out at least five of these pictures. Make sure to cut out their entire bodies. Then cut off the heads. (You will be replacing these heads with pictures of your head and your friends' heads.) Glue the bodies onto different colors of poster board.

6 Make color copies of the photos of you and your friends, or ask permission to cut up the original pictures. Cut out the heads of you and your friends.

7 Now turn yourself and your friends into fashion models, rock stars, or sports celebrities. Arrange the heads on top of the different magazine pictures you cut out in Step 5. Glue in place and allow to dry for 30 minutes. You can create as many images as you want, but make sure you have at least five. Cut all of your new images out of the poster board.

8 Cut different lengths of string, and tape one piece of string to the back of each image. Hang your mobile while you finish this step. Attach the loose end of the string to the wire mobile with a double knot. To balance your mobile, tie one picture to each corner of the mobile and one to the center. You can add more pictures if you like, but be sure to move them around to find the balance point. Now your friends will be able to *hang out* all day and all night!

More Mobile Fun

Cut out from a magazine a picture of a sports car with its top down. Then paste your photo in the driver's seat and your friends' pictures in the passenger seats. Or make all of you part of your favorite rock group! Add these fun group pictures to your mobile.

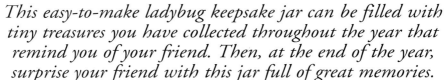

✿ Keepsake Jar ✿

This easy-to-make ladybug keepsake jar can be filled with tiny treasures you have collected throughout the year that remind you of your friend. Then, at the end of the year, surprise your friend with this jar full of great memories.

You Need

• empty glass jar with lid • dish towel • newspaper
• no-baking glass paint in red, black, green, and yellow (found at local craft stores)
• paintbrush • toothpick or blunt pencil (optional) • clear nail polish

Directions

1   Wash the glass jar and lid. Dry as much as possible with a towel. For best results, also let the jar and lid sit out overnight to completely dry.

2   Spread newspaper over your work area. Paint the lid red and allow it to dry for one hour. Remember to wash the paintbrush with soap and water so it will be clean when you switch to a new color of paint.

3   Now create ladybug spots on the top of the lid. Dip the pointed end of the paintbrush into the black paint and then dot the top of the lid. Repeat until the lid is covered with ladybug spots. Let dry for one hour, and don't forget to wash the paintbrush.

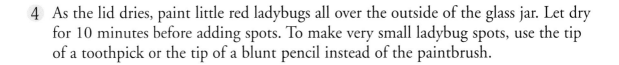

4   As the lid dries, paint little red ladybugs all over the outside of the glass jar. Let dry for 10 minutes before adding spots. To make very small ladybug spots, use the tip of a toothpick or the tip of a blunt pencil instead of the paintbrush.

5 Paint a few yellow flowers and green leaves on the jar. Don't be afraid of making a mistake. With a damp napkin, you can wipe off your mistake and start again when the jar is dry.

6 Let your finished design dry for one hour. Then use clear nail polish to paint a thin coat over the entire design. This will keep your hard work from washing off. If you want to give your keepsake jar to your buddy right away, fill it up with her favorite jelly beans or other fun treasures. Make sure to tell your friend not to wash her keepsake jar for at least a week. This will help the design last longer.

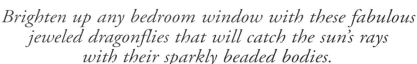

Jeweled Sun Catchers

*Brighten up any bedroom window with these fabulous
jeweled dragonflies that will catch the sun's rays
with their sparkly beaded bodies.*

You Need

• nine silver pipe cleaners • assorted sizes and colors of beads
(the kind that sparkle) • nail clippers • clear nylon thread

Directions

1. Separate your pipe cleaners into groups of three. You will use each group for one dragonfly. Be careful when handling the pipe cleaners, as they have very sharp points.

2. Fold over the end of one pipe cleaner about ¼ inch. This will be the top of your dragonfly. Then thread a large bead onto the pipe cleaner.

3. Working from the bottom of the dragonfly, thread a medium-sized bead onto the same pipe cleaner. Slide it next to the first bead.

4. Take another pipe cleaner from the same group. Bend it in half and twist it onto the first pipe cleaner, right behind the last bead. Then bend it to form wings, and twist it to attach it to the dragonfly body.

5. Thread another medium-sized bead onto the other side of the wings. Bend the third pipe cleaner in half and twist it onto the first pipe cleaner, right behind this last bead. Bend it to form wings, and twist it to attach it to the dragonfly body.

6 Thread three more medium-sized beads onto the first pipe cleaner, then add four smaller beads. Use nail clippers to cut this pipe cleaner about ¼ inch below the last bead. Bend the end of the pipe cleaner toward the bead. This will keep the last bead from falling off. Finish the dragonfly by bending the tail up in a graceful curve.

7 Repeat Steps 1 through 6 to create the other two dragonflies. Make them different by mixing up the beads and experimenting with different colors and sizes. When you're done, cut about 24 inches of nylon thread for each dragonfly. Tie the thread onto the dragonflies' bodies. Hang them near a window. Your friend will probably "bug" you until you show her how to make these adorable sun catchers.

Please Your Buddies with Butterflies

Just for fun, make a few butterflies. All you need to do is grab a couple more pipe cleaners, then form them into antennae and one set of heart-shaped wings. Add them to your existing dragonfly. Your friends will love how these simple jeweled creations brighten up their windows and rooms.

❀ Sweetheart Bracelet ❀

Bits and pieces of clay go a long way when you create this charming bracelet for that special friend.
Adult help needed.

You Need

• waxed paper • $\frac{1}{4}$ block each of white and pink polymer clay • toothpick
• wire • glass baking dish (approved by a parent to bake clay in)
• thin elastic cord • scissors

Directions

1. With an adult, read the handling instructions on the clay package. When you are ready to begin the craft, cover your work area with waxed paper.

2. If the clay isn't soft when you take it out of the package, you can soften it by kneading the clay with your hands. To keep your clay clean, make sure to wash your hands before and after working with each new color of clay.

3. Pinch off a marble-sized piece of white clay and roll it between your hands to form a ball. Repeat until you have five marble-sized balls. Use a toothpick to poke a hole through the center of each ball, turning them into beads.

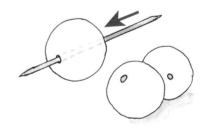

4. Pinch off some of the pink clay and make 10 smaller balls. To turn the balls into hearts, first flatten the balls and shape each one into a teardrop. Shape the teardrop into a heart by using a toothpick to indent the bottom, or fat part, of each teardrop.

5　Lightly press two pink hearts onto each white bead (be sure not to cover up the holes). Carefully roll each bead around to smooth the hearts. The heart shapes will distort a little as they are rolled into the bead, but that's okay.

6　Make five more balls, slightly smaller than the white ones, out of the remaining pink clay. Use a toothpick to poke a hole through each pink ball.

7　Slip the wire through all the beads. Make sure the beads don't stick to the wire. Ask an adult to bake your beads on the wire for 10 minutes at 275 degrees in the glass baking dish.

8　Let the beads cool completely before touching them. After they have cooled, take them off the wire and string them onto the elastic cord, alternating the colors. Knot the ends of the cord together to create a bracelet. Cut off any excess cord. When you are done with your project, wash the baking dish, work area, and your hands.

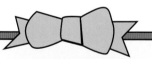

A Necklace to Match!

Now that you are a pro at making clay beads, follow the same steps, but just make a single heart bead and two smaller pink beads. String the heart bead in between the two pink beads onto a long leather cord. Knot the ends of the cord together. Your sweet jewelry just got sweeter!

✤ Ladybug Bubble Fun ✤

*Treat your favorite sidekick to this totally fun
ladybug bubble necklace.*
Adult help needed.

You Need

• newspaper • cup • pencil • red and black acrylic paint
• two paper plates • small sponge brush with handle • small plastic bottle
• 12 inches of 20-gauge wire • small cork (one that will fit plastic bottle)
• needle nose pliers • 1 yard of thin cord

Directions

1 Lay newspaper over your work area. Place the cup on the newspaper, and put the pencil inside the cup. (This will hold your plastic bottle while the paint dries.)

2 Pour a small amount of red paint onto one of the paper plates. Use the sponge brush to paint the small plastic bottle red. Don't paint the bottom. When you're done, set the bottle down on its bottom and let dry for 30 minutes. When it's dry, paint the bottom red, and set the bottle on its top. Let dry for another 30 minutes. This is the ladybug's body. Wash out the sponge brush.

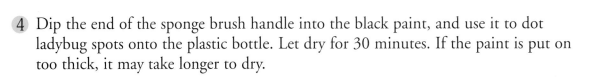

3 Pour a small amount of black paint onto the second paper plate. Use the sponge brush to paint a black line down the ladybug's back. Also paint the lip of the plastic bottle black. Rinse out the brush.

4 Dip the end of the sponge brush handle into the black paint, and use it to dot ladybug spots onto the plastic bottle. Let dry for 30 minutes. If the paint is put on too thick, it may take longer to dry.

5 Ask an adult to carefully bend the wire in half and poke both ends through the bottom of the cork. Push them all the way through the cork so they extend about 2 inches beyond the top of the cork.

6 You may need a parent to help you with these next two steps. With the needle nose pliers, twist the ends poking out the top of the cork into tight antennae swirls.

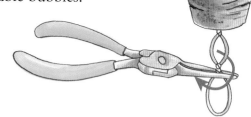

7 Use the needle nose pliers to twist the other ends of the wires to form a double circle for blowing double bubbles.

8 Now tie the cord around the ridge of the bottle to keep the bottle in place. Tie both ends of the cord together to create a necklace. It will now be able to hang around your neck!

9 Put your favorite bubble-blowing mixture inside the bottle. Cork it, slip it around your neck, and set out to have lots of bubble-blowing fun with your friends.

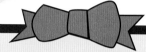

Make It Yourself!

Here's a simple recipe for a bubble mixture: I cup water, ⅛ cup liquid dish soap, and ½ tablespoon glycerin. Gently mix ingredients, then pour into a bottle.

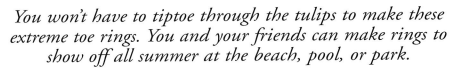

Tiptoe Rings

You won't have to tiptoe through the tulips to make these extreme toe rings. You and your friends can make rings to show off all summer at the beach, pool, or park.

You Need

- 30 inches of beading thread • two beading needles
- various colors of seed beads • towel • scissors • clear nail polish

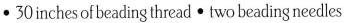
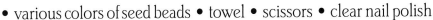

Directions

1 Thread one end of the beading thread through one beading needle. Then thread the other end of the beading thread through the second beading needle.

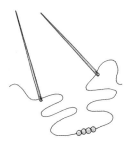

2 Lay your beads on a towel to keep them from rolling. Use one needle to thread four beads of the same color. Slide the beads until they are centered between the two needles.

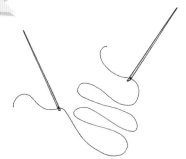

3 Using the same needle, thread four beads of a different color, but before they slide down the thread, use the second needle to thread them from the opposite direction. Gently pull the thread until this second row of seed beads rests on top of the first row.

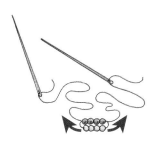

4 Repeat the process until your toe ring is just the right size for your toe.

5 To complete your circle, thread the first needle through the first four beads. Then thread the second needle from the opposite direction through the first four seed beads.

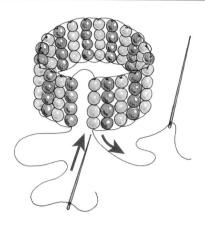

6 Knot the ends of the thread together, then trim them with the scissors. To keep the knot secure, dab a bit of clear nail polish onto it. Let the nail polish dry for 10 minutes before trying on your toe ring.

Go Crazy!

Once you discover how easy these rings are to make, you can experiment with all sorts of patterns and widths.

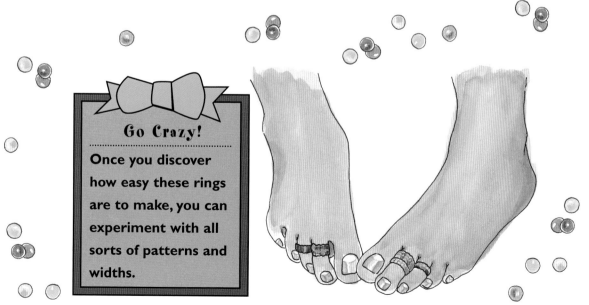

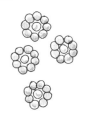

❀ Daisy-Chain Anklet ❀

Your friends will adore this beaded treasure and
probably ask you to make them another and another.

You Need

- beading needle • 30 inches of beading thread • jewelry clasp (found at craft stores)
- white, yellow, and green seed beads • scissors • clear nail polish

Directions

1 Thread the beading thread through the needle so the needle is in the middle of the thread.

2 Then thread the needle through the small needle hole in the clasp. Tie a double knot, but make sure to leave a 4-inch tail of thread hanging from the clasp.

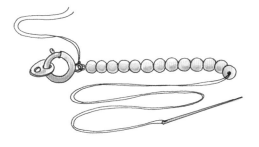

3 Thread the needle through five green beads, which will be the daisy stem. Next, thread the needle through eight yellow beads, the daisy petals.

4 To form your daisy, thread the needle back through the first yellow bead. Gently pull the needle to form your daisy shape. Make sure the beads are snug. Now you are ready to make the daisy center. Thread one white bead, then thread the needle back through the yellow bead that is directly across from the first yellow bead (yellow bead number 5).

5 Repeat Steps 3 and 4 until the anklet is long enough to fit around your or your friend's ankle. To finish the anklet, thread the needle through the end clasp. Double knot the ends, then thread the needle back through the last three beads. Cut off any excess thread, and make the knots secure with a dab of nail polish. Let polish dry for 10 minutes.

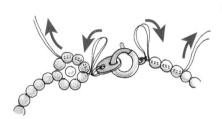

6 Now you want to do with the first clasp what you just did with the end clasp. Thread the needle with both strands of the tail from the first clasp. Thread the needle back through three beads. Cut off the excess thread. Don't stop with just one. Try making another anklet with different-colored seed beads for the daisies.

❀ Friendship Rocks ❀

*Keep your buddy smiling with these unique
paperweights made from ordinary garden rocks that you
decorate to look just like you and your pal!*

You Need

- two smooth rocks (choose rocks with flat bottoms and curved tops)
- newspaper • plastic wrap • white chalk • fine-line colored permanent markers
- acrylic paints (the color of your hair and your friend's hair) • two paper plates
- batting • craft glue • felt square • scissors • yarn (optional)

Directions

1. Wash and dry the rocks. Let them sit overnight.

2. Spread newspaper over your work area. Place the dry rocks on top of the newspaper. Also place a small piece of plastic wrap on top of the newspaper.

3. Use the chalk to draw your face and your friend's face on each rock. If you don't like your drawing, just wipe off the chalk and start over.

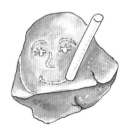

4. Follow the chalk lines with your choice of permanent markers. Don't forget to use the right colors for your eyes and your friend's eyes. If you or your friend wears glasses, draw them on, too!

5. Now pour a small amount of acrylic paint onto one of the paper plates. Take a small amount of batting and pull it apart to make it look like hair. Dip the batting into the paint. Work the paint into the batting by rubbing the batting and paint between your fingers. Let the hair dry on the plastic wrap for 30 minutes. Wash your hands when you're finished. Repeat the process for the other hair.

6 Spread a thin amount of craft glue onto the rock where you want the hair to go. Place the hair on the glued portion of the rock and press down firmly. Sculpt the hair to look like your hair and your friend's hair. If you wear your hair in pigtails, use yarn to tie pigtails. Let the hair dry for one hour.

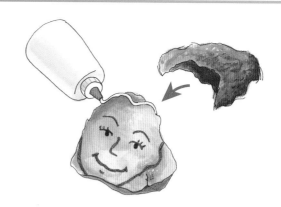

7 To complete your rocks, cut a piece of felt the same size as the bottoms of the rocks. Spread a thin amount of craft glue over the felt and press the felt onto the bottoms of the rocks. Let dry for one hour. Your friend will think that your paperweight gift is not only charming but useful!

FRIENDSHIP ROCKS!

Make It Easy!

To make this craft easier, skip Step 5 and purchase doll hair at your local craft store. Wool or synthetic doll hair will work just as well as the colored batting. You could even use fabric scraps for hair bows. Just glue in place.

Funky Flower Power

Everyone will love this flower-shaped address book.
It's easy to make, and your pals will want to add
their addresses and phone numbers to it.

You Need

- plain paper, at least 4 inches square • pencil • scissors • neon yellow and green stiffened felt (found at craft stores) • cup • strong craft glue • hole punch
- several sheets of 8½ x 11-inch paper in assorted colors • reinforcement holes (found at grocery or office supply stores) • ruler • thin black pen • raffia

Directions

1. Draw a flower design 4 inches in diameter on the plain paper. When you are happy with your design, cut it out. This will be your flower pattern.

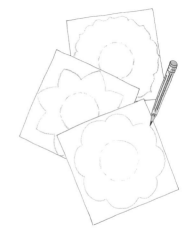

2. To make the cover of your address book, lay the flower pattern on top of the yellow felt. Trace around the pattern with a pencil, then cut out the felt flower. Repeat for the back of the address book.

3. Cut out two green felt circles that are 2 inches in diameter or less. The bottom of a cup will work nicely as a pattern. This will be the center of the flower.

4. Spread a thin layer of glue over one side of a green circle. Firmly press the glued side onto the center of the flower. Repeat the process, gluing the second felt circle to the second yellow flower.

5. Stack the flowers together. Use the hole punch to punch two holes on the left-hand side of the flowers. The holes should be 1¼ inches apart. Try not to punch out any of the green portion of the flowers.

6 Using your flower pattern, now trace and cut out 26 colored paper flowers.

a

b
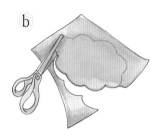

c
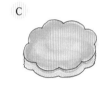

7 Stack four paper flowers together. Using the holes on one of the felt flowers as a guide, punch out two holes on the paper flowers. Repeat until all the paper flowers have two holes on the left-hand side. Place a reinforcement hole onto each paper flower hole. If your paper isn't lined, you may want to use a ruler and a thin black pen to add lines for your friends to write on.

8 Sandwich the paper flowers between the felt flowers. Line up all the holes and secure the address book by threading raffia through the holes and double knotting. Use scissors to trim any excess raffia. Your friends will have a blast adding their addresses and phone numbers to this totally cool address book!

Make It Buzz

Carefully cut one yellow and one black pipe cleaner in half. Pipe cleaners have very sharp ends and can poke, so handle carefully. Twist the yellow and black pipe cleaners together. Wrap them tightly around a pencil and then slip them off. Smash the pipe cleaners down to look like a bee. Then twist on thin black wire for antennae. Glue your creation onto the end of a pen. What a perfect gift to give to a friend along with the flower address book.

Bangle Button Bracelet

*A gazillion tons of fun to make,
this mega-cute bracelet will thrill your best pal!*

You Need

• 14 inches of black elastic cord • masking tape
• lots of shiny metal shank buttons (with the metal loop in the back)
• towel • scissors

Directions

1 Tape one end of the elastic cord with masking tape. This will keep the buttons from slipping off the cord after you've put them on in Step 3.

2 Lay all the buttons on a towel to keep them from rolling around. Then pick out the gold and silver buttons. These are the ones you will need for this project. Place the small gold and silver buttons in one pile and the large ones in another pile.

3 Thread a large button onto the elastic cord, then thread a small button. Repeat, alternating large buttons to small, until the bracelet is full and fits around your wrist.

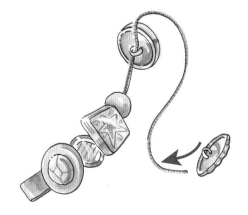

4 Remove the masking tape and double knot the ends of the elastic cord. Use scissors to trim any excess cord. Now give one of your favorite friends this flashy bracelet.

Button Bonanza

Buttons are perfect doodads to dress up many craft projects. Start a button collection, so you'll always have a few on hand. One way to collect buttons is to check with an adult each time he or she is about to throw away an old or worn-out shirt, dress, or pair of pants. If any of the clothing has buttons, first snip them off, then stash them in a place you won't forget!

✿ Personalized String Ring ✿

Your friend will feel adored when you make this personalized ring just for her.

You Need

• string • scissors • two-hole button (size of a penny) • thin black elastic cord • thick marking pen • batting (size of a quarter) • white glue • sheet of patterned tissue paper • newspaper • instant decoupage (found at craft stores) • paper plate • fine-tipped gold liquid paint permanent marker

Directions

1) First, create your friend's initial, which will sit on top of the ring. Cut a small piece of string and shape it into the first letter of your friend's name. The letter should fit completely on the button. If your friend's name begins with a letter such as an *H* or an *A,* you may need to use more than one piece of string. Once you have cut the letter pieces, set them aside.

2) Working from the bottom side of the button, thread each end of the elastic cord through one buttonhole. This is your ring.

3) Slip the ring onto a thick marking pen. This will hold your ring in position while you decorate it. Double knot the elastic cord on top of the button. Use scissors to trim excess elastic.

4) Spread a thin amount of glue on the batting. Wrap the batting around the top and sides of the button. Add more glue if needed. Next, tear the patterned tissue paper into small ½-inch pieces.

5) Spread newspaper over your work area. Then pour a small amount of instant decoupage onto the paper plate. Use your finger to spread a thin layer of decoupage onto the back of one piece of tissue paper. Place the tissue onto the batting. Work quickly to avoid drying. Slip the ring off the pen and smooth the tissue around the sides and back of the ring, getting out any wrinkles. Repeat until three layers of tissue have been applied.

6 While the tissue is still wet, take the string from Step 1 and place it on top of the ring in the shape of your friend's initial. Spread one last thin coat of decoupage over the ring. Slip the ring back onto the thick marking pen and let dry for one hour.

7 Use the gold pen to highlight your friend's initial. This precious ring is a special gift that will jazz up any outfit.

❀ Flutter By ❀

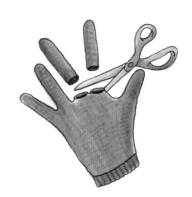

*This precious butterfly finger puppet
will make your heart flutter.*

You Need

• old black net glove (must be okay to cut it) • scissors
• small piece of batting or cotton ball • sewing needle • black thread
• 4 inches of black pipe cleaner • pencil • 8½ x 11-inch piece of yellow craft foam
(found at craft stores) • colored permanent markers

Directions

1. Use scissors to cut off two of the glove fingers.

2. Carefully fill one of the fingers with a small
amount of batting or a cotton ball that has been
pulled apart. Then sew the opening closed with
the black thread. This will be the end section of
your butterfly's body.

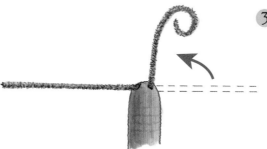

3. Fold the pipe cleaner in half. Working
from the inside of the second glove
finger, carefully push both ends of the
pipe cleaner all the way through the
fabric. Curl the pipe cleaner ends to look
like the butterfly's antennae. This will be
the butterfly's head.

4. Slip the sewn end of the
first finger ¼ inch inside
the second finger. Sew the
first finger to one side only
of the second finger,
leaving an opening.

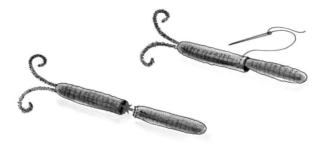

5 Use a pencil to draw large butterfly wings on the craft foam. Cut out the butterfly wings with the scissors.

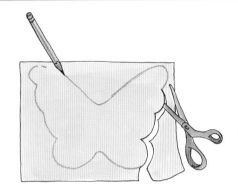

6 Following the illustration below, cut two 1-inch slits into the butterfly's wings. The glove—now the butterfly's body—will need to fit through the slits in Step 7. Decorate the wings with colored markers. Let dry for 10 minutes.

7 Starting with the end section of the butterfly, weave its body through the slits in the butterfly's wings. Slip your butterfly puppet onto your finger and let your butterfly flutter by!

Jeepers Peepers

Did you know that stylish Americans spend more than $2.5 billion dollars a year on sunglasses? Well, you'll look like you paid a million bucks for these cool shades.
Adult help needed.

You Need

• old pair of large-framed sunglasses • lots of colorful buttons
• paper • pencil • low-temperature glue gun and glue sticks

Directions

1 Carefully wash the sunglasses with mild soap and water. Dry thoroughly.

2 Pick out the buttons you like best. Vary the sizes and colors of the buttons.

3 Place the sunglasses on top of the paper and use the pencil to outline their shape. Lay the buttons on top of the outline of the sunglasses frame in a pattern you like. When you're happy with your design, use the pattern as a guide to help you glue the buttons onto the real sunglasses.

4 With an adult's help, use the low-temperature glue gun to carefully glue the buttons onto the frame of the sunglasses. Do not cover up the lenses. Overlay the buttons one on top of the other. Make sure to decorate the front of the arms of the sunglasses. You will love your customized sunglasses—and so will all your buddies!

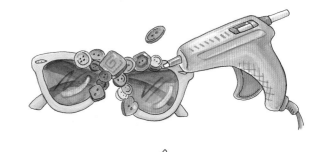

Classy Glasses

Here are a couple more ideas for decorating another pair of shades: Make cool designs with neon-colored puffy paints. (This looks especially cool on black sunglasses.) Your whole face will sparkle if you glue glitter on your glasses, either in tiny polka-dot patterns or zany stripes.

❀ Hanging Flower Basket ❀

*If you have a pal who needs cheering up,
this nifty basket of posies should do the trick.*

You Need

- newspaper • cone-shaped paper cup • two sheets of flower-patterned tissue paper • instant decoupage (found at craft stores) • paper plate • craft stick • 24 inches of silk cord • stapler • gold pen • small ball of clay • small silk flower bouquet • dried green grass (found at craft stores)

Directions

1 Lay newspaper over your work area. Place the cone-shaped paper cup— pointed side up—on the newspaper.

2 Tear the tissue paper into small pieces. Pour a small amount of instant decoupage onto the paper plate. Working quickly (decoupage dries fast), use the craft stick to spread a thin layer of decoupage over a 3- to 4-inch portion of the outside of the paper cup.

3 Then quickly place the torn tissue pieces over the section of the paper cup with the decoupage. Use your finger to smooth. Repeat, overlapping tissue until three layers have been applied. Let dry for 30 minutes before moving to the next part of the cup. Repeat this process until the entire cup is covered with tissue.

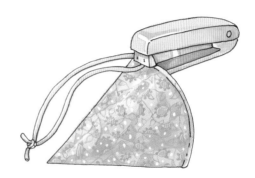

4 After the flower basket has dried completely, fold the cord in half and knot the ends together. Create a handle by stapling a loop of cord on one side of the flower basket.

5 With a gold pen, write your friend's name in fancy letters on the front of the flower basket.

6 Now place the clay ball into the bottom of the cup. Stick the ends of the silk flower bouquet into the clay to keep the bouquet secure. Arrange the dried grass around the flowers in the basket. Hang your beautiful flower basket on your friend's doorknob. It will be fun to watch her guess which crafty friend made her such a classy gift.

❀ Dress Up with a Tie ❀

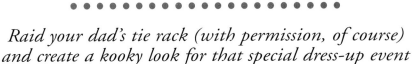

Raid your dad's tie rack (with permission, of course) and create a kooky look for that special dress-up event you're having with your friends.

You Need

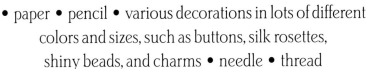
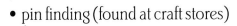

• ruler • old tie • scissors • craft glue
• paper • pencil • various decorations in lots of different
colors and sizes, such as buttons, silk rosettes,
shiny beads, and charms • needle • thread
• pin finding (found at craft stores)

Directions

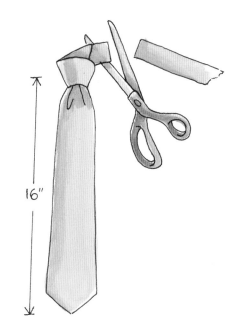

1 Use the ruler to measure 16 inches up from the bottom of the tie. Tie a knot here. Use scissors to cut off the unknotted portion of the tie. (You can make a second tie from this piece.)

2 Tuck the cut side of the tie under and glue in place. Also spread a thin layer of glue inside the knot to hold it in place. Press down on the knot for a few seconds, then let dry for one hour.

16"

3 Use the pencil to trace an outline of the tie onto the paper. Lay the buttons, beads, and other decorations on the paper in a pattern that you like. Use this as your guide for Step 4.

4 Thread the needle. Sew the buttons, rosettes, beads, and charms onto the tie, completely covering the entire tie. Glue the pin finding onto the back of the tie near the knot. Let dry overnight before wearing. What a groovy gift to make and receive!

Ties Aren't Just for Boys!

Other things that you can make with an old tie:

- Cut the tie in half lengthwise and use it as a headband or hair ribbon.

- Cinch the tie around your waist for a groovy belt.

- Hang the tie on your wall and attach all your jewelry pins and clips to it for safekeeping.

It's easy and fun to create a batch of these zany beady kids.

You Need

- assorted beads • towel • 28-gauge wire
- scissors or wire cutters • needle nose pliers

Directions

1. Place the beads on top of a towel to keep them from rolling around. You will need a medium-sized bead for the head, a flat or starflake bead for the collar, two long beads for the arms, two small beads for the cuffs, one large bead for the body, four long beads for the legs, and two small, flat beads for the pant cuffs.

2. Use scissors or wire cutters to carefully cut one 7-inch and one 10-inch length of wire. Fold both wires in half.

3. With the folded ends first, thread both folded wires through the head bead. Push both wires out 1 inch. Fold the wires over to keep the head bead in place.

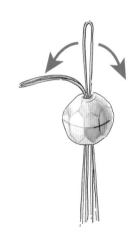

4. Thread the flat bead or starflake bead (used here) for the collar onto all four wires. Slip it under the head bead. Crisscross the two shorter wires, then bend one wire to the left at a 90-degree angle and the other wire to the right at a 90-degree angle. These wires will be the arms.

5 Thread one long bead onto one arm wire, then thread one small bead onto the same wire for a cuff around the hand. Use the needle nose pliers to bend the end of the wire into a small loop for the hand. Thread the wire back through the small bead. Repeat for the other arm.

6 Thread the large body bead onto the two remaining wires. Next, pull these wires apart to keep the body bead from slipping off.

7 To create the legs, thread two long beads onto one of these remaining wires. Then thread one small bead for the pant cuff. Use the needle nose pliers to bend the end of the wire into a small loop for the foot. Thread the wire back through the small, flat bead. Repeat for the other leg.

8 Finally, use the pliers to curl the wires coming out of the head into a flip or pigtails. Try making a few more beady kids using beads of different colors, shapes, and sizes. You can even try to make some to look like a few of your friends.

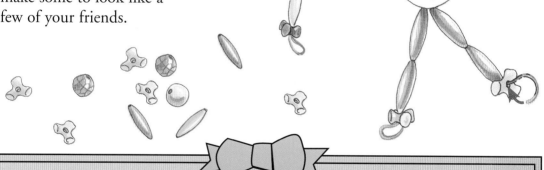

Did You Know?

In prehistoric times, people used beads to buy and sell things. The more beads you had, the wealthier you were. Beads were also used to ward off evil or to count prayers. Some beads were made out of bones, shells, and bug legs, while others were made out of gold, silver, and semiprecious stones. Today, we use beads mostly for jewelry, but some countries still use them for trade.

✿ Daisy-Chain Earrings ✿

Dazzle your friend with this pretty daisy-chain ear gear.

You Need

- 40 inches of beading thread • one pair of earring hooks
- beading needle • 12 green, 16 yellow, and 2 white seed beads
- clear nail polish

Directions

1. Tie one end of the beading thread to the loop in one earring hook. Your knot should be 4 inches from the end of one thread.

2. Thread the other end of the thread through the beading needle.

3. Thread six green seed beads for the daisy stem, then thread eight yellow seed beads for the petals.

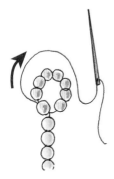

4. To form your daisy, thread the needle back through the first yellow bead. Gently pull the needle to form your daisy shape. Make sure the beads are snug. Now you are ready to make the daisy center.

5. Thread one white bead, and then thread the needle back through the yellow bead that is directly across from the first yellow bead (yellow bead number 5). Loop the needle around the thread and knot. Trim off any excess thread.

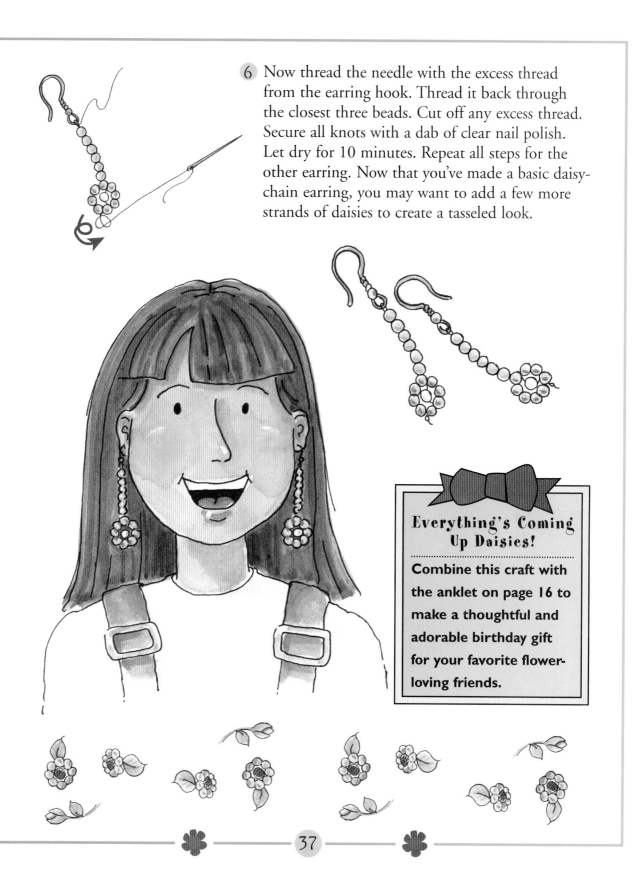

6 Now thread the needle with the excess thread from the earring hook. Thread it back through the closest three beads. Cut off any excess thread. Secure all knots with a dab of clear nail polish. Let dry for 10 minutes. Repeat all steps for the other earring. Now that you've made a basic daisy-chain earring, you may want to add a few more strands of daisies to create a tasseled look.

Everything's Coming Up Daisies!

Combine this craft with the anklet on page 16 to make a thoughtful and adorable birthday gift for your favorite flower-loving friends.

❀ Chummy Zigzag Card ❀

*Show someone just how much you care with
this jazzy friendship card.*

You Need

- one long, narrow piece of heavy colored paper (any color) • ruler
- pencil • empty ballpoint pen • plain paper • colored markers
- magazines • old greeting cards • pieces of wrapping paper
- assorted colored paper • old photos • glue stick

Directions

1. Lay the long piece of heavy colored paper on your work area. Use the ruler to measure the length of the paper. Divide the paper into six or seven equal parts. Lightly mark the parts with the pencil.

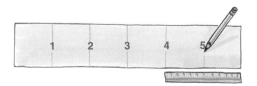

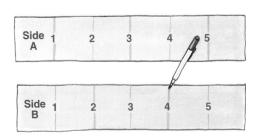

2. Using the pencil marks as a guide, score the fold lines by pressing an empty ballpoint pen along the lines. On side A, score lines 1, 3, and 5, and on side B, score the alternating lines, such as 2 and 4. It will make the next step easier.

3. Fold the paper into an accordionlike zigzag pattern.

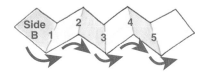

4. On a separate piece of paper, write out what you want each square on your zigzag card to say. You don't even have to use words. You could use pictures to tell your friendship story by using photos from old magazines, greeting cards, comics, or by creating your own pictures from colored paper.

5 For example, one page could have a picture of kids riding their bikes together with the words "Riding bikes with you is my favorite thing to do!" The next page could have two kids eating ice cream out on the front porch with the words "Everything tastes better when you're with a friend!"

6 Once you have figured out what you want to say and how you want to illustrate your card, start cutting, gluing, and writing on the card.

7 Your friend can display the unfolded card tacked to her bedroom wall, or she can keep it on a table with a pretty ribbon wrapped around it.

Make an Envelope

To complete your package, grab a white or manila envelope to fit your card. Decorate the outside of the envelope to match your card. Now you're ready to give your gift away!

Funky Sun Visor

On the hot days of summer, block the sun—
not the fun—with this adorable visor that you
and your best buddy can make together.

You Need

• ruler • pencil • paper • scissors • orange, yellow, and green craft foam
• black permanent marker • strong craft glue • hole punch
• 12 inches of black elastic cord

Directions

1 Using the illustration here as a guide, measure and draw the visor and flower patterns on the paper and cut them out.

2 Place the visor pattern onto the orange craft foam, trace it, and cut it out. Next, place the flower pattern onto the yellow craft foam. Trace three flowers and cut them out.

3 Place the flower center pattern onto the green craft foam. Trace three centers and cut them out.

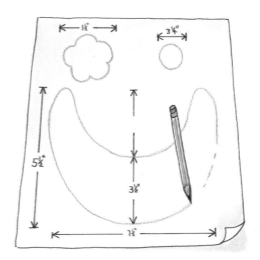

4 Use the black permanent marker to draw a happy face on each flower center. Glue the flowers onto the orange visor. Glue the flower centers onto the flowers. Let dry overnight.

5 Use the hole punch to create a small hole at each end of the visor. Thread elastic through the holes and tie the ends into a double knot. Slip the visor onto your head, and now you are ready to hang out all day at the beach or the pool with the gang.

Get Crafty

If you want to make another visor and you only have a few minutes, try attaching your favorite stickers all over it.

❀ Pillow-Tee Pals ❀

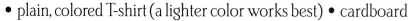

*Decorate a plain T-shirt with pens, buttons, and bows
and turn it into a treasured throw pillow.*

You Need

- plain, colored T-shirt (a lighter color works best) • cardboard
- scissors • pencil • paper • colored fabric pens • needle
- thread • buttons and bows (optional) • fiberfill

Directions

1. Wash the T-shirt with soap and water. Dry in the dryer.

2. Cut the cardboard to fit inside the T-shirt, then slip it into the shirt. This will keep the fabric pens from leaking through to the other side.

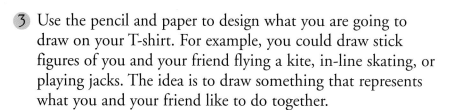

3. Use the pencil and paper to design what you are going to draw on your T-shirt. For example, you could draw stick figures of you and your friend flying a kite, in-line skating, or playing jacks. The idea is to draw something that represents what you and your friend like to do together.

4. Once you draw your design on paper, sketch it in pencil on the shirt, then ink it with the fabric pens. Don't forget to decorate the sleeves and the back of the T-shirt. When you're finished drawing, remove the cardboard.

5 If you plan to use this pillow for your head, you may want to skip this step. But if it's for decoration only, you can sew on some colorful buttons and bows to make the pillow even cuter.

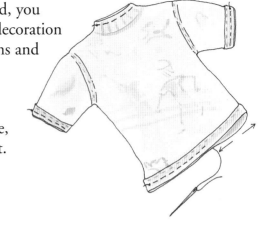

6 Now turn the T-shirt inside out. Thread the needle, and sew together the neck hole, sleeve holes, and the bottom of the T-shirt. Leave a 5-inch opening at the bottom of the T-shirt for stuffing it.

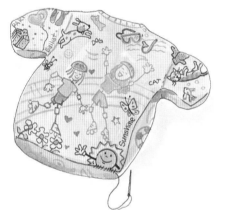

7 Turn the decorated T-shirt right-side out and stuff it with fiberfill. Use the needle and thread to close up the opening at the bottom of the shirt. Now you have a great pillow for any room!

Sleep-Over Fun

This would be a fun pillow to bring to sleep-over parties. Just leave off the buttons and bows (they are too hard for your head), bring a fabric pen to the sleep-over, and have your buddies autograph your personalized pillow.

❀ "Over the Rainbow" Mug ❀

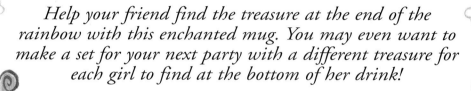

Help your friend find the treasure at the end of the rainbow with this enchanted mug. You may even want to make a set for your next party with a different treasure for each girl to find at the bottom of her drink!

You Need

• newspaper • heavy clear glass mug • paper • pencil • scissors • tape • various colors of no-baking glass paints • clean Styrofoam egg carton • fine-tipped paintbrush • clear nail polish

Directions

1. Spread newspaper over your work area. Carefully wash the mug with soap and water in the sink. Dry it completely.

2. First, you need to draw the design you want on your mug on a piece of paper. To make sure your design is the right size for your mug, roll the paper up and place it inside the mug. Use a pencil to mark where the paper overlaps. Also mark where the top of the mug meets the paper.

3. Take the paper out of the mug, and use the pencil marks as guides for cutting the paper to size.

4. Draw your design on the paper strip. You can follow the rainbow design that's illustrated, or make one up on your own.

5 Once you're happy with your design, slip the strip of paper back inside the mug. You will see your design through the glass. Tape the paper in place inside the mug.

6 Pour small pools of different-colored paints inside the different egg carton compartments.

7 Following the design you drew, paint on the outside of the mug. Let each color dry for 10 minutes before adding a new color. Also make sure to wash out your paintbrush with mild soap and water before switching colors.

8 Finally, flip your mug upside down and paint a pot of gold on the outside bottom. Or, draw another "treasure" that you will find each time you empty your special mug!

9 To make your design last longer, paint over your masterpiece with clear nail polish. Add your name to the mug and don't use it or wash it for six days (this will give the design time to set). *Remember:* Don't wash this mug in the dishwasher. Only wash it by hand.

❀ Flower Box Clock ❀

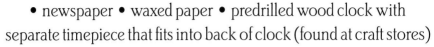

Dazzle your friends with this clever,
one-of-a-kind clock.
Adult help needed.

You Need

• newspaper • waxed paper • predrilled wood clock with
separate timepiece that fits into back of clock (found at craft stores)
• white craft glue • paper plate • sponge brush
• blue, yellow, green, pink, red, and purple polymer clay
• old rolling pin that is no longer used for food
• craft knife • pen • toothpicks
• old baking dish that is no longer used for food

Directions

1. Lay newspaper over your work area, and then spread waxed paper over the newspaper.

2. Place the wooden clock frame (without timepiece) on top of the waxed paper. Pour a small amount of glue onto the paper plate. Use the sponge brush to spread the glue all over the clock frame (except on the bottom, because you won't be placing clay there). Let dry for two hours. Wash out the sponge brush with soap and water.

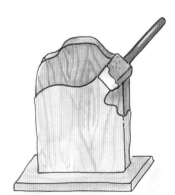

3. Now lay a clean piece of waxed paper over the newspaper. Take out the polymer clays and knead them with your hands until they are soft enough to use. Make sure to wash your hands each time you work with a different color.

4 Use the rolling pin to roll out a thin sheet of blue clay. It should be big enough to cover the wooden frame. Wrap the clay over the frame, pressing it hard against the wood. Don't cover the bottom of the wooden frame. With an adult's help, carefully trim off any excess clay with the craft knife. Wash and dry the roller. (*Remember:* This rolling pin should not be used for food after being used on the clay.)

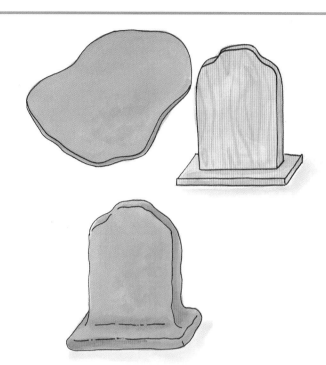

5 To make the sunflower, roll out a thin piece of yellow clay. With an adult's help, use the craft knife to cut out separate sunflower-shaped petals. Create a circle of overlapping petals by pressing the petals lightly onto the blue clay to cover the clock frame. Wash and dry the roller.

6 To make the center of the sunflower, roll out a thin piece of green clay. With an adult's help, use the craft knife to cut out a circle smaller than the sunflower. Lightly press the bottom of a pen into the clay to create small seed imprints. Place the center of the sunflower in the middle of the sunflower petals. Press in place. Use a toothpick to create a hole in the center of the sunflower for the timepiece to slip through.

7. Use small, flat pieces of different colors of clay to create the numbers 12, 3, 6, and 9 for the clock. Press the numbers onto the clock face (the green center of the sunflower).

8. To make other decorative flowers, roll out four tiny balls of clay. Put the balls in a circle. Use your finger to flatten the balls. Next, make a flower center out of different-colored clay. Roll the clay into a tiny ball and place it in the center of the flattened balls. Press it into place by gently flattening. Make as many decorative flowers as you like.

9. To make a flower leaf, roll out a tiny ball of green clay. Flatten the ball and pinch one end with your fingers to form a teardrop shape. Use a toothpick to create leaf veins. Pinch the rounded end of the leaf to finish it off. Make as many leaves as you want.

10. To make a ladybug, roll out a pea-sized ball of red clay. Flatten the ball slightly and use your fingers to shape it into an oval, like a ladybug. Then roll out a tiny ball of black clay for the head. Press the head against the ladybug's body and partially flatten. Press a toothpick into the ladybug's back to create a line down its back. Shape teeny-tiny balls of black clay for the ladybug's spots. Press them onto the ladybug's body and lightly flatten.

11. To make a butterfly, roll out two pea-sized balls of any color clay and two slightly smaller balls into four separate wings. Roll a small rope of clay for the butterfly's body. Place the body on waxed paper with the rolled-out pea-sized ball on top of one side and a small-sized ball beneath. Repeat for the other side of the butterfly. Press the balls down lightly. Pinch the bottoms of the small balls to create a nice butterfly wing. Use other colored clay scraps for color on the wings.

12 Press the flowers, leaves, ladybug, and butterfly wherever you want them on your clock. Then get ready to bake your clay. Have an adult read the handling instructions on the clay package before baking. Ask him or her to bake the clock, sitting upright, in an old glass baking dish for 20 minutes at 275 degrees. Have an adult take it out of the oven for you. The clock will be *very* hot! When the dish cools, wash it.

13 Follow the clock directions for installing the clock piece. You may want to give this sweet flower box clock to a special friend to let her know you think about her every hour of the day.

❀ Freeze Frame ❀

Turn old jewelry, trinkets, and buttons into a fresh 'n' funky frame for your favorite buddy.

You Need

- newspaper • waxed paper • 6½ x 8-inch frame mold (found at craft stores)
- pencil • paper • old jewelry • trinkets and buttons • large plastic container
- measuring cup • art plaster • 6 ounces warm water
- old large mixing spoon • acrylic paint • frame back (found at craft stores)
- glue • photo of you and a friend

Directions

1. Lay newspaper over your work area. Lay an 8 x 10-inch piece of waxed paper on the area of newspaper on which the plaster frame you make will dry.

2. Use the pencil to trace the frame mold onto the paper. You'll use this drawing as a guide for placing your objects in the plaster.

3. Lay the jewelry, trinkets, and buttons on the paper frame in a pattern that you like.

4. Pour 12 ounces art plaster into the plastic container. Add 6 ounces warm water to the plaster, and mix together with a spoon. Stir until the mixture is smooth like pancake batter. Next, add a squirt of acrylic paint and stir well. If you want a marbled look, swirl the paint with the spoon instead of mixing. If your frame is larger or smaller, you will need to adjust the amounts. (It's usually a good idea to make a little more plastic mix than you need to be sure you have enough.) Slowly and evenly pour the plaster into the frame mold.

5 The plaster will begin to set in 10 to 20 minutes. Using your drawing as a guide, press the jewelry, trinkets, and buttons into the plaster before it gets too hard (the plaster should feel firm, not hard). Be careful where you place your objects, because you don't want to reposition them. When you have completed placing your objects into the plaster, use one end of a toothpick to create swirls in the plaster (without disturbing the objects). Make sure not to pour any plaster down the drain—it can clog it. Throw away extra plaster in the trash.

6 Let the frame sit for three hours, then carefully take it out of the mold. It will still feel a little damp. Place the frame onto the waxed paper and let dry for 24 hours. Take the frame back apart, and spread a thin layer of glue onto the back of the frame back. Press the frame back firmly onto the back of the plaster frame. Let dry for one hour.

7 Slip a picture of you and your buddy into the frame, and then sandwich it with the second piece of the frame back. Your friend will be thrilled with your gift and with you for making it so special!

Theme It!

Go with a theme. If your friend loves the ocean, have someone take a picture of the two of you in the surf. Then create a frame with various seashells and ocean charms. You can even buy colorful plastic charms in many different shapes, including dogs, cats, baseballs, and soccer balls.

❀ Catch the Wind ❀

This heart-shaped wind chime will catch more than the wind—it will capture your friend's heart.
Adult help needed.

You Need

- newspaper • waxed paper • wire clothes hanger • pliers • white acrylic paint
- paper plate • sponge brush • oven-baked clay (found at craft stores)
- old rolling pin • two wooden rulers (optional) • heart-shaped cookie cutter
- pencil • fishing line • scissors • raffia

Directions

1 Lay newspaper over your work area, and then spread a piece of waxed paper on top of the newspaper. Hold the hanger just below the hook with one hand. Ask an adult to help you use pliers to grip the bottom section of the wire and pull it down to form the bottom point of the heart.

2 With your hands, push in the sides of the wire.

3 Then push down the center of the wire to create a heart.

4 Pour a small amount of white paint onto the paper plate. Use the sponge brush to paint the wire heart white. Let dry for one hour.

5 Have an adult help you read the directions on the back of the oven-baked clay. Roll the clay out onto the waxed paper to ¼-inch thickness. Rolling the clay out in between two wooden rulers should give you this thickness.

6 Press the heart-shaped cookie cutter into the clay and cut out three hearts. Use a pencil to poke a hole in the top of each clay heart. *Remember:* Don't ever reuse cookie cutters on food after they've been used on polymer clay. Store any leftover clay scraps inside a zip-top bag.

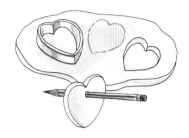

7 Follow the baking instructions carefully on the back of the clay package. Most clays will need to dry out for a day or two before you can bake them. Have an adult help you bake the clay. The adult should remove the clay from the oven, as it will be very hot.

8 After the baked clay hearts have cooled completely, thread the fishing line through each hole and attach each heart to the center of the wire heart. Vary the length of the fishing line to stagger the hearts, but keep them slightly touching, so they'll hit each other.

9 Tie a raffia bow right under the wire hook. You can hang your wind chime in a tree or out on the patio.

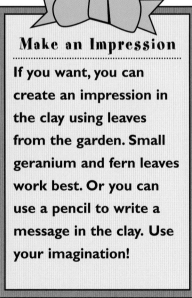

Make an Impression

If you want, you can create an impression in the clay using leaves from the garden. Small geranium and fern leaves work best. Or you can use a pencil to write a message in the clay. Use your imagination!

❧ Places to Go ❧

*Travel to exotic destinations with this place mat
covered with all the places you and your friend
have dreamed about visiting.*

You Need (for each place mat)

• photo of you and friend • newspapers • old magazines • scissors
• 12 x 21-inch piece of plain paper • 15 x 25-inch piece of cardboard
• clear contact paper • four thumbtacks • rolling pin

Directions

1 Cut out a photo of you and a friend (make sure to ask permission first).

2 Then, with your friend, thumb through the travel sections of the newspapers and some old magazines. Cut out the pictures of the places that the two of you would like to visit together.

3 Lay your pictures on the plain paper in a pattern that you like. Use this as a guide for arranging the pictures on the contact paper.

4 Now place cardboard on your work area.

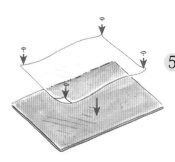

5 Cut out two 12 x 21-inch pieces of contact paper. Peel off the paper on the back of one piece of contact paper. Then lay the contact paper on top of the cardboard, sticky side up. Use the four thumbtacks to keep the contact paper in place.

6 Arrange your pictures on the contact paper, using your practice sheet of paper as a guide. When you like what you see, carefully take out the four tacks. Then peel the paper off the second piece of contact paper and place it over your travel collage, sticky side down. Use a rolling pin to press out any bubbles in the paper.

Make a place mat for both you and your friend, and then while you're eating your cereal, you can both dream about all the places you want to see!

Don't Stop There

Once you and your friend visit the places that are on your place mat, gather together photos, postcards, and other travel trinkets and create a new place mat. This one will be about all the places that you and your friend have already seen together!

❀ Cinnamon Kisses ❀

This simple recipe for cinnamon heart and lip ornaments will make any room smell good enough to eat.

You Need

- waxed paper • cutting board
- 1 cup ground cinnamon (can be bought cheaply in bulk)
- mixing bowl • mixing spoon • ³/₄ cup applesauce
- 1 tablespoon white glue • rolling pin • heart- and lip-shaped cookie cutters
- blunt pencil • ¹/₄-inch spool of ribbon (any color) • scissors

Directions

1. Lay waxed paper on top of the cutting board.

2. Pour 1 cup ground cinnamon into the mixing bowl. Be careful not to breathe in the cinnamon powder.

3. Use the mixing spoon to add ¾ cup applesauce to the cinnamon.

4. Then add 1 tablespoon white glue to the mixture.

5. Stir the cinnamon, applesauce, and glue together. If the mixture gets too dry, add more applesauce. If the mixture gets too wet, add more cinnamon. The mixture should be stiff like dough. When you're done mixing, let the dough sit in the bowl for 10 minutes.

6. Sprinkle a little ground cinnamon onto the waxed paper, then knead the dough on the waxed paper. If it begins to stick, add more cinnamon. Don't rub your eyes after handling the cinnamon or the dough. Make sure to wash your hands well with soap and water when you are finished.

7 Use the rolling pin to roll the dough out as thick as a standard pencil. Press the heart- and lip-shaped cookie cutters into the dough. Cut out as many ornaments as you want.

8 Use a blunt pencil to poke a hole at the top of each ornament. The hole should be large enough for the ribbon to thread through. Let the ornaments air dry for 24 hours. To keep them from curling, turn them over after 12 hours of drying.

9 After the ornaments have dried completely, thread on some ribbon. Make the ribbons different lengths and tie a cluster of ornaments together into a bow. Your gift may smell good enough to eat, but make sure your friend knows it is only for her nose and eyes to enjoy!

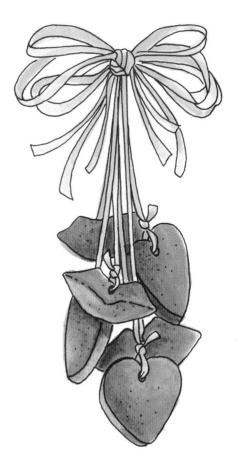

Munchtime

Give your friend the munchies with this kooky hamburger and fries. No onions, please!

You Need

• pencil • paper • scissors • craft foam in medium and dark brown, yellow, red, and green • brown, yellow, red, and green acrylic paints • fine-tipped paintbrush • paper plate • craft glue • plastic wrap • glue stick • black pen

Directions

1 Trace the food and bag patterns onto the paper. Cut them out with scissors.

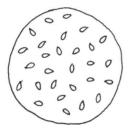

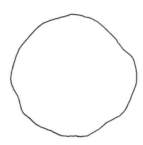

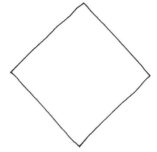

2 Place the food patterns onto the appropriate colored craft foam. Outline and cut out the foam shapes. Remember to make two hamburger buns, meat, lettuce, tomatoes, cheese, and lots of skinny fries.

3 Use paints to paint details on the craft foam food. For example, you can paint sesame seeds on the hamburger buns, veins on the lettuce, and ketchup on the fries. Let dry for 15 minutes.

4 Glue the hamburger pieces together. Let dry for 20 minutes. To keep the foam hamburger pieces from sticking straight out, wrap the hamburger up tightly in plastic wrap. Keep the hamburger wrapped up for one hour. Repeat the steps for a plateful of hamburgers.

5 Cut out a tiny paper plate from a big paper plate. Stack your hamburgers on the plate.

6 From the paper plate, cut out a french fry bag. Fold the straight edge of the french fry bag over ¾ inch. Then unfold the bag and spread a thin line of glue from the glue stick along both sides (leave top open for french fries). Fold the straight edge back over ¾ inch and press down to hold in place. Let dry for 15 minutes.

7 Write FRIES on the outside of the bag. Slip the fries into the bag. Glue them in place if needed. Add your bag of fries to your plate of hamburgers. Hmmmm, if you only had a soda!

Buddy Blooms

*Create a garden of smiles with this miniature flowerpot
and colorful photos of you and a sidekick.*

You Need

• pencil • paper • scissors • heavy colored paper
• individual photos of you and your friend • craft glue • toothpick
• moss • small ball of clay • 1-inch miniature clay flowerpot

Directions

1. Trace the flower patterns onto the plain paper and cut them out. Place the patterns onto the colored paper. Outline them with a pencil and cut them out. You need two of each pattern. In one of the two, cut out the center to fit a photo.

2. You will need one photo of your face or a friend's face for each flower. If a photo face is too big to fit in the center of the paper flower, make a photocopy to shrink it down. Use scissors to cut out each face so it fits in the center of the flower.

3. Spread a thin layer of glue over the parts of the flower that don't have the center cut out.

4. Place one end of a toothpick ¼ inch down from the top of the glued flower. Place the photo in the center of the flower. Place the second flower piece (the one with the center cut out) on top of the photo, sandwiching the photo and toothpick. Press down hard. Let dry for 10 minutes.

5 Spread glue across the remaining section of toothpick. Sprinkle moss onto the toothpick. Let dry for 10 minutes. Tie a long, thin scrap of fabric onto the flower stem to create leaves.

6 Place the small ball of clay into the bottom of the flowerpot. Stick the toothpick flower stem into the clay. Fill up the pot with moss. It may be tiny, but it's big on CUTE!

Angel Baby

Make a jeweled felt angel to watch over your dearest friend.

You Need

- pencil • paper • scissors • 9 x 12-inch champagne-colored felt
- strong white craft glue • 4-inch-long gold elastic loop • acrylic paints
- fine-tipped paintbrush • batting • chopstick • clothespin
- 125 white iridescent sequins, 12-mm size
- doll's hair or lamb's wool • 14 x 1-inch gold metallic wire ribbon

Directions

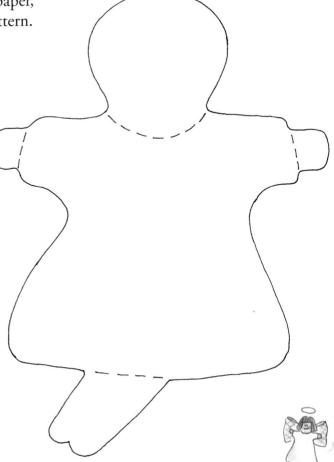

1. Trace the angel doll outline onto paper, then use scissors to cut out the pattern.

2. Place the pattern onto the felt. Use the pencil to outline the pattern. On the back, mark this piece A. Turn the pattern over and outline it on a second piece of felt. Mark this piece B on the back. Use scissors to cut out both pieces.

3. Use a pencil to lightly outline the angel's dress (see the dotted lines on the example) on the side of the fabric that isn't marked A or B. Repeat on the second piece.

4. Run a thin bead of glue along all the edges of side B, leaving a 1-inch gap where you will insert the stuffing. Lay the gold loop at the top of the head. It should stick out 1 inch for hanging the angel. Then place piece A on top of B, the glued piece. The gold loop will be sandwiched between A and B. Press hard to secure, then let dry for two hours.

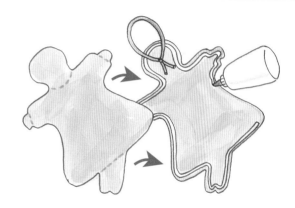

5. While the glue is drying, use paints to add detail to the angel's face. To create the eyes, dip the bottom of the paintbrush into the paint and dot on the eyes. Paint fingers, then outline the legs as shown. Let dry for 30 minutes. Next, paint the backs of the fingers and legs.

6. Gently stuff the angel with batting. Use the chopstick to get the stuffing into the head, arms, and legs. When you're done, close up the opening with glue. Secure it closed with a clothespin. Let dry for one hour. Remove the clothespin.

7. Spread a thin layer of glue around the edge of the dress. Place sequins on top of the glue. Spread more glue next to the first set of sequins, then add another row of sequins, overlapping them with the first row. Continue adding sequins until the dress is covered. Let dry for one hour. Repeat this step to decorate the back of the angel's dress. If the glue is layered on too thickly, it could take longer to dry.

8 Glue the doll's hair or lamb's wool onto the angel's head. Let dry for one hour.

9 To make the angel's wings, lay the 14-inch ribbon flat. Fold one side of the ribbon to touch its center. Fold the other side so it overlaps the first. Now twist the center. Glue the angel's wings onto the back of the dress, just below the head. Let dry for one hour. Your friend will think you are an angel for making her this heavenly gift.

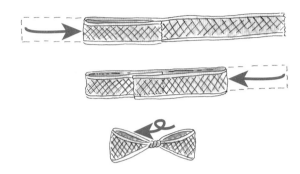